T0208028

Nursing Your Marriage 24/7
She Can Do It, He Can Help

A Nurse's Perspective
after 39 Years of Matrimony

By
Betty H. Ali

Nursing Your Marriage

24/7

She Can Do It, He Can Help

A Nurse's Perspective after 39 Years of Matrimony

Betty H. Ali

Rev. date: 11/17/2017

To order additional copies of this book, contact:
Xlibris
1-888-795-4274
www.Xlibris.com
Orders@Xlibris.com
770588

Dedication

To my mother and father, *Pearl Godfrey Hill and Moses Hill,* who did the best they could to raise their five daughters and one son

To my nephew, *Ali Williams,* most high forever, we love you

To my wonderful sister, *Jan Pearl Hill,* who will be alive in my heart and mind forever

To my husband, *Brother Kareem,* who never broke his marriage vows

Acknowledgments

Special thanks to *Dr. Chanda Pilgrim* for contributing to this book.

Special thanks to my book editor, *Yemi Toure*. His eye for detail and his judgment were invaluable. He added greatly to the quality of the work, but all of the conclusions are my own.

NOTE TO READER:

Readers will notice many broad statements that may not apply to all individuals. People often talk in broad generalizations. I could write the way people talk, or I could load the book down with cautions, exceptions and reservations.

I wanted to connect with readers, so I chose to write in the more conversational, down-to-earth fashion. I chose to write the way many people talk.

- Betty H. Ali

Table of Contents

Foreword

FINDING BALANCE

By Betty H. Ali

I never considered reading a book on love and marriage.

For me, the start of the process seemed simple enough—have a boyfriend, start dating, have fun. Thank goodness my big sister told me that I could get pregnant, a subject never discussed at my home.

Three years later, I had a husband and a baby. Definitely life-changing. I had to find the balance between all the elements.

Key:
Balance

Marriage Survival Prayer

Keep love in my heart always

Show me the way

And guide me to be

Nonjudgmental

Give me the strength

To go with the flow

Not against the grain

Of the peace in my life

Prologue

In The Beginning

By Brother Kareem

In New York in 1975, when I met the woman who was to be my wife, I had already experienced plenty of relationships. These women were crazy about me. But I was not at all crazy about them.

I met Betty, my future wife, at a dance in Manhattan. She mimicked all of my dance steps. After we danced, I moved around the club, looking for my next prey.

I fit the profile of what women desired, a well-dressed, well-mannered man, smelling good.

Later that evening I danced with another lady. She was more my type. She was "thick," a meat-and-potatoes woman. As the dance ended, I searched for that "thick" young lady. I could not find her.

Instead I ran into Betty again. She was trying to catch a taxi. We exchanged words for about forty minutes. I asked for her telephone number. She refused, but then later I asked for it again and attempted to kiss her on the cheek. She finally gave me her number.

I went to my aunt's house in the Bronx that night. I told her about my encounter with this female from Harlem. She was concerned. "You just can't go to Harlem and start dating their women. You have to be careful over there."

So when I did go to visit Betty, I took my cousin with me, just in case I ran into any trouble.

This was my first time in East Harlem. I found it to be nice. The people were progressive and smooth. I liked the vibes that I felt from Harlem residents. Then I noticed that there were lots of pretty women in Harlem.

My future wife had a wonderful family. They invited me over for dinner. But I noticed they were serving pork chops. This I had a problem with. At that time, I was in the Five Percent Nation, a self-improvement organization. The eating of pork was restricted from our diet.

At that time, Betty was the lead singer of a popular female group called Pure Essence. I went to most all of her shows. I was impressed.

Two years later we had our first child out of wedlock. We decided to get married after that.

I went into business with my wife's brother to support our new family.

My wife breastfed our new child. And we received lots of child-rearing advice. One health professional told us that if my wife would continue one hundred percent breastfeeding, she could not get pregnant. We believed her, but it was not true—our second child was conceived six months after our first.

My wife still had a lot of energy. She was out enjoying her life. When I came home from work, she was not always at home. I preferred that she be at home. But now as I reflect back, I learned that people need to have their own space. It was a good thing for her and our relationship because everyone needs their space. And if you have something in your system, it's better to get it all out.

Once my wife settled down, she returned to college. I supported her every step of the way.

We decided to move to Atlanta. We immediately went apartment hunting, and found a four-bedroom, three-bath, fully-carpeted apartment for $500 a month, where the first month was rent-free.

The apartment complex had a swimming pool. This was heaven on earth. We were excited and overwhelmed with joy.

I didn't want to leave my immediate family in New York. But I was looking at the big picture. Once my family was settled in Atlanta, I was going back to move my mother down to Atlanta with us.

I did miss New York. I enjoyed taking long walks down those busy streets. It was therapy. When my wife and I had heated arguments, those long walks lowered my stress and anxiety. I was able to walk away from various situations and calm down.

Marriage was one of the most difficult challenges that I have ever faced. It's hard to keep it together, but easy to fall apart.

I had to have skill, knowledge, information and the blessing of God. One tool I used to empower myself was to read books and magazines on love and relationships.

I loved my wife. This made all the difference in the world. I didn't have eyes for anyone else. There are lots of pretty women in the world, but love should be stronger than temptation.

Cheating on my wife would have been wrong. It required too much energy and stress. Ducking, dodging, hiding, lying. I could lose my children, house and wife, over a fifty-minute sensation. I would have to put a sensation over something I loved.

If I did, I would have broken the marriage, and had restrictions on seeing my children. I would lose more than I gained. I have seen this happen too often to men from every walk of life.

Also, I was worried because I grew up without my father in my life, and I wanted to be certain that my children grew up with me in their lives.

So love is the key. Love allowed me to have much more tolerance. And there was much that I had to tolerate, such as female hormonal ups and downs, which contribute to mood swings.

Communication is also an important skill that is needed in marriage. I could not read my wife's mind, so I had to improve on my ability to communicate.

Also, timing is everything. "Should I discuss this matter now? Should I do it in person or over the phone?" Very important.

Patience is another skill I had to develop. Many women are emotional creatures. They need to be taken care of, protected, secured, made comfortable and taken out to eat. Time must be spent with them. You can almost compare it to taking care of a precious gift.

I do not mean to be offensive because women are our first teachers and we all came from a woman. So I do honor women.

This is the commitment that is needed. And many young men don't realize this. There is a lot involved in having a long and loving marriage.

But when it is all said and done, marriage is a beautiful thing. It makes a man whole and complete.

So I take it one day at a time. I may be upset today, but I will feel better tomorrow.

chapter 1 |

HUMAN BEHAVIOR

When I was in nursing school, my regular classes were tough. But I also took the time to study psychology. This was a God-send when it came to my marriage.

All women—and men—should learn about human behavior, especially how information is processed in the mind. We should also learn more about how to deal with different personalities and emotions.

We are men and women first, and husband and wife second. I learned that you have to allow a person to express how they feel. Let them get it all out. Let them finish what they are trying to say. They will feel better after. They will be calmer, and then you can speak. This will allow for better communication.

Another option is to seek out advice from aunts or uncles or other relatives who have been married a long time. (But don't ask for advice from Aunt Belinda, who just got divorced for the fourth time!)

However, if communication stays poor and you find that a marriage counselor is necessary, please seek out help. This is a good thing, a good thing, and a good thing.

The man's perspective and the woman's perspective are both important when receiving counseling. If you have a counseling team, that would be even more beneficial.

Key:

Know how to listen.
Don't react with emotion––it's better to act with intelligence.

chapter 2 |

KNOW EACH OTHER

had to get to know the person I was falling in love with before I fell too deep. It takes time to really know a person (maybe two years or longer, and if you live with a person, you learn even more about them). At this stage I was on the phone with my mate constantly. Asking questions, investigating––does he have a job? Is he in school? Does he have a bank account, children, child support payments? What are his plans, aspirations, goals, etc.? Do his actions match up to all the things he tells me? Actions speak louder than words.

Also, I paid attention to how he treated his mom and dad. If he didn't respect them, he wouldn't respect me in the future, no matter how much he smiled today.

This gathering of information helped me to know my future husband better. It took time and energy.

Some may not like to do this information-gathering, but it should be a normal part of the courtship process for each partner. It is a basic compatibility assessment of one another.

My mate passed the assessment test. I also liked the fact that he brought his mom a small gift whenever he could.

When Brother Kareem was 16, his dad came back into his life. So during his young life, he lacked the positive "male role model." He would always say that he beat the odds and is blessed to still be alive.

My husband was always well-dressed. My dress style was plain and simple. He would purchase cloth for me to improve my wardrobe. And he always took me out to dinner.

We took long walks though parks. As we held hands, I could feel the electricity flowing from his hand through mine. This to me was magical.

Keep in mind that in my future husband's neighborhood, he was still popular with the ladies. They were after him. I was at his home one day when a young woman riding a bike knocked at his door. I later found out that she traveled 20 miles to get to his home. WOW! So she knocked and knocked and knocked. Of course the knock was ignored.

This situation did not bother me at all because he and I were together almost all the time.

When we lived in New York, I had two older sisters who had boyfriends. We would go visit my sisters sometimes. They would coach me on what to say on the phone to Kareem. They told me to ask him to buy me things. He would buy everything that I asked for. My sisters thought he was handsome and RESPONSIBLE. They placed their stamp of approval on him. That's what big sisters did.

There was one area that he needed to focus on, which was completing the 12th grade. We both knew that this was important. We discussed it, and he returned to school, graduating with a diploma.

The main thing one must know is whether the man truly loves you, which is demonstrated best by a person's actions, not words alone. This is a must. This is what stood the test of time for our relationship.

Love helped us to go the extra mile. If someone told me my husband was cheating, that would not be enough. I had a rule—"I have to see it for myself." This would be concrete evidence for me. I never saw it in 35 years. And I didn't go looking for anything.

Key:

Actions speak louder than words.

chapter 3 |

Study Each Other

We had to study each other's likes and dislikes. This helped us avoid arguments. We had to remind each other about this, what we liked and what we didn't, but reminders should be given with a warm spirit.

That old slogan is true—it's not what you say, it's how you say it. And always remember that patience is a virtue. A long-term marriage is based on many things, one of which is give-and-take on both sides.

To study someone takes time and patience. And don't forget that people have faults that only manifest over time. Trial and error should be expected.

I learned not to react to everything that WARRANTED a reaction. Many times, silence WAS golden.

One challenge for me was my husband's lack of facial expression. His emotions could change five times, but it was hard to tell just by looking at his face.

This made it difficult for me to read him emotionally. This is still a challenge for me.

But this was not just on his side. One of the first nonverbal expressions that I had to take control of was jealousy. This emotion can spiral out of control and can cause major confrontations and violence. Learn it, know it, stop it!

I had to also study my husband's point of frustration. Of course I could ignore it and win many verbal battles. Many women can do that well. But I learned that sometimes it's better to just RETREAT. YES, this is an excellent strategy that is not used enough. It works. And knowing when to retreat is crucial. Timing is definitely EVERYTHING.

If we got into a really heated argument, it was best for someone to take a walk. Someone had to calm down before it got physical. I knew my husband enough to know when it was time for the exit strategy.

I tried to admit when I was wrong. This was also one of the best things to do.

Here is one thing that drove me nuts and still does today. I can fix myself a sandwich and ask my husband, "Honey, would you like a sandwich?" He would say "No." He would wait until I put all the food away, and then he would say, "Oh, can you make me a sandwich?" It was like clockwork, EVERY TIME. Go figure—and call me when you do. So

I fix the sandwich and fuss at the same time. Now I just always make two sandwiches.

In talking to other women about men, they would say men are like babies, like having another child. Now it is all starting to make sense. No comment on whether it's true.

In my study, I would seek out advice from other couples who have been married longer than I have. The one piece of advice they all gave me was to give each other personal space. No one wants someone sweating them all the time.

Key:

In a marriage, be ready to compromise.

chapter 4 |

Understand Each Other

Understanding my husband played a big part in our relationship. Men from different parts of the country are good at different things. My husband is from New York City, the "Concrete Jungle." When we got our house in Atlanta, it needed handiwork. This was a big problem. Kareem was not from a Southern state, where many men are good at handiwork, and this was his first home. I argued with him at first about fixing things around the house. Then we compromised and decided that if he couldn't fix something himself, he would pay someone to do it.

So we solved the problem of fixing things up around the house. But then we had the problem of messing things up around the house. In other words, I could not understand why my husband would do certain things. (The understanding part always seemed to hit me at a later time.)

Like why would you put on my new slippers to take out the garbage in the rain and mud? Not good at all.

At first I wanted to scream and yell at him, but he was in the shower at the time. So I knocked on the door, went in, pulled the shower curtain and kindly stated, "Honey do you have any idea how my brand new slippers got soaking wet?"

"Oh, I'm sorry," he said, "I was just trying to take out the garbage."

I wanted to throw the slippers at him! I was heated. I walked out of the bathroom and said nothing more.

Remember I said earlier that understanding would often hit me at a later time? Here is what hit me about the slippers––my husband never considered that my fluffy slippers would get messy and soak up all that water.

I think I will buy him a pair of slippers.

Another part of understanding your mate is family history. I believe kinfolk play a major role in influencing personality. So be sure to consider your mate's family before making a commitment.

When correcting your mate, positive reinforcement is the best approach. Here is an example where I did not use positive reinforcement: "You were wrong when you told our son to get up so early and cut the grass before his exam."

And here is what I could have said: "Honey, our son was up until very late last night studying for his exam. He should have let you know that, so he could rest this morning."

Too often, we are quick to say what we don't like about our mate, and slow to say what we do like. But verbalizing what we enjoy about one another is the best way. This helps us to build a stronger relationship.

You have to analyze the faults and habits of your mate, seek to change the things you can, then decide if you can deal with the others for a lifetime. If you accept them, don't complain later. You accepted them, so now work it out.

Key:

Understand your mate's strengths and weaknesses.
Help each other grow.

chapter 5 |

TRUST EACH OTHER

Trust was a big issue for me to cope with. My husband owned a business selling women's apparel in New York. OF COURSE I HAD CONCERNS about other women hitting on my husband, and they did. Now this is where the love part is put to the test. DANGER ZONE—HOT WOMEN. If he loves me, he will navigate through this temptation. I had to trust him.

Society tells us that men are dogs. So why should I trust my husband? "Some men are dogs, and when they stop being dogs, then we can trust them."

Trust for me is what joined our hearts together. It is that unseen power that also requires some faith.

Here is another example of trust. When my husband said we were going to leave New York and move to Atlanta, I was surprised and worried. He stated that he did his research. And he said we needed a bigger living space.

I was pregnant with my third child. I didn't think the timing was right. I felt trapped.

He asked me to trust him because he had it covered. So I had to trust his judgment. He played his role as a man. King of the throne. (Trust me, men love this stuff. You know, being king.)

My husband comforted me and stated that he would be there for me, take care of me and help me through it. Yes, I had fears, but thank God he kept his word, and he still does till this very day. I can't speak on what might happen tomorrow.

He did the best that he could. And that's all you can ask for. He has been a great husband, father and friend.

Another key trait that my husband demonstrated was strong initiative. That "get up and go...," "let's get it done...," "make it happen...," spirit. This is not something to take lightly, because if we didn't have much materially, that spirit of initiative reinforced the hope that I could hold on to.

I always pray to God that I remember to count my blessings. And not be ungrateful. Because surely too often, humans are ungrateful.

Key:

If you are looking for trouble you will ALWAYS find it.

chapter 6 |

SUPPORT EACH OTHER

The nature of a man is different from the nature of a woman. And because our natures are different, we have two different roles to play. When you understand your roles, this leads to a successful marriage. Case in point: In the 21st Century, some women are out working and men are home taking care of the children. But the man's nature is to be the breadwinner. So always know that he is the king no matter what position he might be in.

Women have become very successful in the corporate arena, but we should not look down on our mates. We should support our mates by being a good help meet. Always be careful not to belittle his manhood.

Instead make him feel needed. He holds the key. He has insight. He helps the family to flourish and prosper. (The last four sentences: These equally apply to women.) He is significant, even if this society doesn't tell you so.

During tough times, women may have to be responsible for all the financial obligations in the home. But this is what teamwork is all about. Yes, you are a team. Help him until he can get back on his feet. He should be working hard toward getting himself together. He should also start to help you around the house a little more.

Because the black man is Public Enemy Number One in society, he should receive some support at home. His home should be his sanctuary. Please don't put unnecessary pressure on him. We must be a cushion of support.

Key:

Let a man be the man. Let him feel needed.

chapter 7 |

Forgive Each Other

very human being has faults. These faults become obvious as a marriage grows, so expect them. That's why too many marriages fail in the early years, because couples are not willing to compromise. In my own case, I was trying to create the perfect picture, but marriage is not picture-perfect (duh!). This is where forgiveness comes in.

I was speaking with a psychologist, marriage counselor Dr. Sakinah Rasheed. She stated that forgiveness was a major component to a successful marriage. We must forgive our mates.

My husband is not strong in every area of his life. And I am not strong in every area of my life. Because we are not strong, we all make mistakes. Sometimes they are really big mistakes that really hurt. It can make you feel like you are losing in a boxing match.

So it is not surprising that in that boxing ring of the heart, sometimes you get knocked around.

But, like Muhammad Ali, you have to be flexible so you don't break.

It can be difficult to bounce back from such injury. But forgiveness helps you bounce back. Forgiveness, like love, lives inside the chambers of the heart. They hang out together. So keep them both in your heart.

When I hurt my husband, I also hurt inside. Then I ask for mercy so that he can see through his pain to forgive me.

In 1999, we made a $3,000 purchase. At that time Kareem's credit was better than mine, so he signed for the item. I promised that I would pay half the bill. Three years went by and I did not keep my end of the bargain. This destroyed my husband's credit rating. As we attempted to purchase other items on credit, he would get turned down. I was totally crushed. I was to blame because I did not keep my end of the deal.

I really had good intentions. But that's not good enough. Should he forgive me? Why should he? I needed to handle my business. I needed to fix this problem that I created. He never screamed or yelled about it. Can you imagine that?

He did forgive me. So today, if I can't afford to buy something outright, I will wait and purchase it when I can.

Key:

God can forgive us, thus we should forgive each other.

chapter 8 |

MINIMIZE ARGUMENTS WITH EACH OTHER

difference of opinion will always be an issue. In my own case, I had to learn to disagree without being disagreeable.

And that is easier said than done. It took skill, practice and patience. I first had to evaluate the situation. I had to make improvements in being nonjudgmental. I had to focus more on making my husband feel special.

You might want to focus on a surprise gift for your mate. Tell him all the wonderful things you appreciate about him. And he should do the same for you.

If we have a heated argument, my husband will be the first to offer an olive branch of peace. He takes the time to explain and analyze exactly what happened. This is a very important step to resolving the issue. This makes all the difference in the world. Opening up communication is the key.

I am the opposite. I am stubborn and will not speak to him for a week. And that is not a good thing. I learned that no one is guaranteed today or tomorrow.

In addition, my husband has another tactic he uses to settle down our big heated arguments. He would stop in his tracks and state, "Look, this problem is bigger than you and me. Satan is always working, and we can't let him win!"

We would both calm down, blame it on the devil and forgive one another.

It worked––most times––like clockwork. However this approach did not fit every situation.

Sometimes the devil successfully worked through my husband. And he was to blame on that day.

Key:

Keep the channels of communication open.

chapter 9 |

LOVE EACH OTHER

I asked my husband why some men say they make love to some women but have sex with others. He said that some men can perform the mechanical act of sex and feel no emotional connection to that female afterward. Many men will lie, tell a woman he loves her, tell her what she wants to hear. Words are easy to say.

But ahhh, making love. He said men make love to women they really are devoted to, that they really care about.

So a key word here is devotion. It is the glue that holds the marriage together. He has to show you that he is devoted to you through his actions, reactions and transactions.

Love is the healing force of the world. How did we stay married for 35-plus years?

One thing is certain––my husband was in love and did love me. This was a major factor, along with our strong belief in the Creator that we serve.

I also loved him. But my loving him alone––or his loving me alone––would not be enough to hold a marriage together. It's the man being in love with the woman, and the woman in love with the man. This, I think, is one of the prerequisites for a long-lasting marriage.

Key:

Love is wanting what is best for each other.

chapter 10 |

Now Add Children

When children were added to the equation of our relationship, everything changed.

Now we had to re-evaluate our time management strategy. Children pulled me away from my private time, personal time, study time, vacation time. And my husband was also time-challenged.

Our entire lifestyle was overhauled. I was now split three ways. My only hope would be to create a weekly routine schedule with a print-out, and stick it on the refrigerator. I had to improve my organizational skills. And I bought many parenting magazines and followed their great ideas and solutions.

Parenting contributed to additional mental stress. It was important to know when I needed a mental break because I really did not want to take my frustrations out on my children.

Parenting is like your own REALITY SHOW with drama, horror and comedy. But, unlike the TV reality shows, we always should strive for a happy ending.

———————————————————

Key:
Organize yourself.

chapter 11 |

Keep Yourself Together

After all is said and done, from dealing with the husband, children, cooking, shopping, cleaning, laundry, doctors' appointments, baseball practice, dance class, etc., one element of paramount importance is that I had to keep myself well-groomed. Especially when my husband walked through that door after a hard day's work.

I could not look like Tired Susie Home Maker, or Need A Weave Jane. And remember, my husband was well-dressed and well-mannered, no matter what kind of day he had. So I had to do my part.

One routine that allowed me to transition into Part Two of my day was a quick 20-minute nap. This helped minimize my stress and maximize my tolerance.

I had to change my clothes and fix my hair. This is what attracted him to me in the beginning. I had to keep it going. Amen from the men's corner.

In addition there is competition from women on the hunt. I didn't get it twisted to be listed as the Mrs. who lost all her kisses.

Key:

Take time for yourself in your own way.

chapter 12 |

MENTAL HEALTH

Some men are possessive, obsessive and dominating! You may not see these traits at the beginning, but you may see hints of them. I had to be like a detective, taking notes of important information. I recommend going on the Internet and searching for Mental Health - Signs and Symptoms. You can't then go diagnose your husband, but if you have an idea of what to look for, you can get professional advice about how to handle it. Some people may have family members with different types of mental illnesses. So seeking advice is not a bad thing; just something to consider.

In addition, take time for yourself, just you alone; take a mental health break. Down time, "me time," just time. This will help to maintain your balance or mental tolerance level. I enjoy taking a nap sometime during the course of the day. And don't forget to go on vacation every chance you can.

SO NURSE YOUR MARRIAGE. IT MAY HEAL YOUR RELATIONSHIP!!!

NURSING MEANS NURTURING-- ENCOURAGING SOMEONE TO GROW, DEVELOP, THRIVE, FLOURISH AND BE SUCCESSFUL.

Afterword

THE FIVE C'S TO A SUCCESSFUL MARRIAGE

By Dr. Chanda Pilgrim

Introduction

The second part of this book is a commentary on how to create a successful marriage.

The first thing is that it is vitally important to have God in your relationship. I am not one to say a particular religion, but it is important to understand that we were created to be paired, and that the answer to all problems we have can always be solved by the Creator, who is responsible for our daily breath.

It is important to spend time renewing your spirit together. If that means church, or mosque, or temple, or meditating at home... however you and your partner choose... just do not forget to look to the spiritual teachings that are available to you. (If you don't do the religion thing, but are still interested, there are many books that have detailed information about the perspective of God in relationships.)

The second thing to keep in mind (and it is the foundation of this book) is that there are three sides to any story—his view of the truth, her view of the truth, and the truth. If you are aware of this fact, keep in mind that no matter what it is you think, feel or believe, there may be another way of looking at things. If you do this, then you are open to the realization that there are certain unspoken laws and keys to success in marriage. The following section is dedicated to helping you recognize them and learn how to use them.

The Five C's

When I talk to people about the laws to a successful marriage, I discuss the Five C's: Communication; Compromise; Caring; Commitment and Consummation. Let's discuss them.

Communication

This is something that seems so easy. In the beginning of a relationship, you spent a lot of time talking; it was how you got to know one another. Yet many people say problems with communications are what caused their marriage to fail. The reason is that communication is more than just talking; it is also listening to what the other person is saying.

Often when we become mad, we are only interested in getting our point across. We are not hearing what the other person is saying. Communication must be both people taking turns talking and listening. You must be aware of when the other person can't hear any more, and you must stop. This is called the saturation point. Anything you say beyond the saturation point is not heard.

A friend of mine who is a marriage counselor, Gloria Cunny, told me about a technique to help a discussion not turn into a fight. The person who is speaking holds a piece of carpet or something to represent the floor (the floor meaning person "has the floor" to speak). The person who is listening holds a sponge and will squeeze it when they cannot listen and process any more information. Now, once the person squeezes the sponge, the mate does not try to get any last points in— you are wasting your time, it will not be heard.

That is the point of the floor and sponge technique, so you can know when your partner can no longer hear what you are saying. You may find that this technique can help with the perception of being nagged, because you are given the opportunity to explain why you feel that way and you can tell how much of what you said is actually heard. This way both people feel like they have control over what is happening in the conversation.

Also, whenever you are talking to your partner, be sweet, like you were when you were not married. Everyone wants to feel good. Allow your partner to be your partner, your helpmate, your friend, not another rival. Your house should be a refuge from all the trials of life.

There is an unspoken issue of respect here—when you are talking and you do not feel like your partner is hearing you, don't you feel like they are disrespecting you? You must stop and ask yourself if you are getting your point across clearly. Explain what is happening, how you feel, but don't turn it into nagging. Nagging is another example of not paying attention to the saturation point.

Compromise

Once you have really listened to what the other person has said, you have to find the common ground between the two of you. If your partner feels so strongly about something and it's not all that important to you, please, give in. Likewise, when you are passionate about something, and your partner is noncommittal, it is time for your partner to give in. You must remember that there must be give and take. If one person is doing all the compromising, at some point that partner may become resentful, which leads to a myriad of problems.

Caring

A topic often on people's lips is falling in love and falling out of love. Falling in love is what happens early in a relationship; it is what brings you together emotionally; it is the "chemistry" between two people. Once that time has passed, and the butterflies flutter only occasionally, does that mean it is time for a divorce? Absolutely not. That is when true love starts growing. True love is caring for someone completely. It is wanting what is best for your partner, no matter what. When you truly care about someone, you help them to be the best person they can be. You help each other to grow toward your mutual goals.

Commitment

This is probably the biggest quality missing in marriages today. People stay committed as long as things look, smell and sound good. Once the challenges start, the sentiment is, "I don't have to put up with this mess... I'm out of here." While there is some "mess" that you do not need to put up with (examples are abuse and adultery), couples can really work though many of the issues that they are faced with. It is the commitment to the marriage that gives you the staying power. You may be angry, annoyed, fed up with something. But it is that desire to make things work that keeps you together.

Consummation (Sex)

This is last but definitely not least. I know some of you out there are saying, "Yeah, I like that one," and you should—it is a big part of a marriage. When things are going well, it may not matter if you go for some time without sex. However, when the relationship is having its challenges, a lack of sex becomes a major issue. When I discussed the Five C's with my father (who has been married to my mother for 41 years), he said that the consummation piece is important because it is the time when you renew your love for one another. It is the time when all problems disappear, when nothing else matters but you and your partner. Now I am not saying that sex will make problems go away. (I know some of you have tried that already.) Sex may postpone the problems temporarily (depending on how big the challenge), but it will not get rid of them.

This leads me to the next problem. There are those ladies out there—you know them—who get mad at their husbands and decide to punish them by withholding sex. While this may appear to solve the problem sometimes, it is definitely NOT a solution. I have heard too many times a man say, "If I can't get it at home, I know plenty of willing women who will gladly take care of my needs." If you are lucky enough to come from a marriage where the man is too committed to the marriage or God to do that, you are lucky.

Infidelity is often, but not always, a reason to leave a marriage. My advice is to determine if it was a one-time thing, or a long-term thing, and what the motivation was. In other words, was it a "heat of the moment" thing, or is it a lifestyle choice? If it is the latter, then it really may be a reason to leave, because things will probably not change. The only possible way that things could change in the second scenario is, if there was some reason for looking outside the marriage, and you can manage to change something about yourself that makes that need no longer necessary.

What do I mean by that? If your husband really wants someone who speaks to him in a certain manner and that turns him on, and you haven't done it for years, and he has started looking outside, you can draw him back home by being that person again. Remember first to look at ourselves before we start blaming our mates, to see if there is anything that we are doing to push our man away. (Are we nagging too much? Are we being supportive?) I am not saying that gives the man an excuse to cheat, or that it is your fault, but try not to create those situations that makes another woman more desirable than you.

This also brings me back to the topics of Communication and Compromise. Men, if there is a problem at home, if you need something different or are not happy, you must talk about it with your wife. She has to know what the problem is if you need her to fix it. Often I hear men talking about the need to have their mate "get at them." Honestly, women are often so busy with work and children, that they may not have the thought or energy to do that. They may still think you are the sexiest man alive and want to be with you always, but life just gets in the way. I recognize the need to feel wanted and that there are plenty of women who may be paying attention to your manhood; however, give your wife the opportunity to be that woman by showing her what you need.

For the man who may be faced with a wife who is not faithful, much of my advice is the same. However, it looks much different to a man. Whereas a woman may forgive her husband, thinking "that's what men do," a man is struck with a hard blow to his ego or his manhood. Therefore, my advice to you, is to try to leave the anger out of it. That may mean you may need a "time out." Walk away, go to Mom's house for the weekend, find some way to calm down so you don't react on that anger.

When you have had a chance to get some perspective on the situation, you need to ask yourself (and her) what has been missing in the relationship. Have you been able to provide financially the way she needs you to? Are you giving her the attention that she needs? (How is that communication going?)

The next step may be to look for a counselor who can help you sort through all the emotions that are going on in your mind and heart. Asking for help is not a sign of weakness. We all have a need to take care of ourselves physically and emotionally. Women often talk to their girlfriends, and are often more willing to go for counseling than men.

Men, holding those emotions inside can be dangerous. It can lead to disease and is often part of the reason that suicide rates are so high for men. PLEASE talk about it before you do something rash.

It may not seem like talking is important, or it may not seem like talking will get you anywhere. But that depends on what the goal of "anywhere" is. If your goal is to get you out of a crisis state and to help you to gain some perspective, then it will most definitely help. Counseling cannot magically make the pain go away or make things different. It does give you a different way of looking at things. The end result may be that the marriage cannot be saved, but it is much better to be able to come to that decision from a calm place than from an emotional place. That reduces the regrets. Marriage is supposed to be a lifetime commitment, so the same way you should take care of your body when it is sick, you should take care of your marriage if it is sick.

Now, let's look at the keys that were highlighted in this book.

Keys to a Successful Marriage

You can look back through this book for the little keys. They highlight the lessons to be learned from each chapter. I will elaborate on some of them here.

Know How to Listen
Be sure that when there is a problem, that you don't react with emotion––act with intelligence.

In the section above I spoke about the importance of communication and being able to listen. If your mate is yelling at you, the chances are that you are not listening to what is being said. When something happens, you must listen to your mate—take time to think about it before your respond. That is what acting with intelligence means. It is making sure that what you are saying is bringing you closer to your goal, whatever that may be.

Actions Speak Louder Than Words
I know you have all heard this one before. Looking at someone's actions tells really what you can expect when you really don't know your new love. If the person says one thing and consistently does the opposite, you can bet that they are only telling you what they think you want to hear. Now why would someone do that? From my experience, the answer often is... to get you or to keep you.

The problem is this: When you discover that the person is truly not who they claim to be, there is often less room for forgiveness. Please also remember to check yourself—are you living up to the reality factor? Do you say what you mean, and live by what you say, or are you trying to please someone or afraid they may leave?

An important litmus test to a man's actions is, "How does he treat his mother?" If he talks about treating you like a queen, but tells his mother, "Stop asking me for stuff all the time. I have my own life to live"—the chances are that once you start having needs and must ask for things, you may hear a similar response.

Also, see how his parents treated each other. Generally, you learn how to be a wife from watching your mother and how to be a husband by watching your father. If you didn't have the role models around, was there anyone who taught you that role? If not, chances are that you learned how to be a husband/wife from television, radio and friends' advice. But those sources come with their own problems. Ask yourself where you got your model for spousal relationships. If it wasn't from a successful marriage, you may have to spend some time relearning how to be a good spouse.

In a Marriage, Be Ready to Compromise
As we have discussed in the previous section, commitment is about stick-to-itiveness. Do you have the staying power? Are you willing to fight for the right to be married? I do not think that there is a marriage (especially those longer than a year) that has had no challenges; it is inherent in the relationship. However, it is how you deal with those challenges that matters. You have to decide that being married is more important than the struggles that could tear you apart. Communicate and compromise so that both partners are happy.

What do we teach our children about love and marriage? Often we don't even think about the need to say anything. As a result, they learn from our example (good or bad). So where does that leave the 50 percent of children who were raised in single-parent homes? Where do they learn about relationships? The scary answer is that they learn often from the media and their friends. Too often we take advice from our friends, who give us a heavy dose of their own reality.

My advice: When you talk to someone who is not a professional, make sure that they have a successful relationship (married at least eight years). At that point in a relationship, most couples have already learned how to negotiate the obstacles that all marriages face. They have learned who their partner is and what they realistically can expect and not expect.

The first year of a marriage is often a mix of the joys of being a newlywed, and the challenges of learning how to blend two individuals, from two DIFFERENT families, into one cohesive family. During this time, it is critical to really LISTEN to the things your partner is telling you. This is how you learn your partner's expectations, how they react in various situations, what they think, how they put their values into practice. This is the "getting to know you" stage.

You must be careful not to delude yourself into thinking you can change someone—you can't! Love doesn't make someone change. You can't expect that "if he really loves me, he would change" or "if she really loves me, she would change." That is not realistic.

Change can only come from a choice that the individual makes, and with the assistance of God. You can ask, show, even prove the need for change, you can even be willing to help them make the change; but the choice can never be yours (even if it is truly the right choice).

If you force someone into trying to change, they will not be committed to the change and therefore, the change won't last. When you love someone, you accept their faults and help guide them. You don't just criticize them. Ladies, men have enough to fight with outside the home; support your man, don't give him yet another fight (even if you are right).

Now I am not saying that you should encourage and accept things that are not correct, but try not to fight about it––that almost never makes a man change his mind. Calmly explain your point of view when your partner is not upset (he will not hear you if he is upset).

Men, you also need to support your mate. A soft tone and a kind deed will soften most women. (Ladies, this can ease men, too.)

Understanding
Understanding can only come from learning who your partner is, listening to him or her and asking questions. Assumptions are a recipe for disaster. Men and women very often do see things differently. Teach him/her how you think. Just because something is obvious to you

does NOT mean it is obvious to your partner. They may really have no clue how you feel.

Remember the incident with the fluffy slippers in Chapter 4? Most men don't know about fluffy slippers; Brother Kareem was just trying to put something on quickly so he could take out the garbage. To him, the slippers served a purpose; that is all. To you, they were something different—soft, fuzzy, comfy slippers when you want to feel somewhat pampered. There are many similar examples of how things are perceived differently. The differences could be based on gender, family upbringing, culture. All families are unique, and all individuals are unique, and everyone has their own way of doing things. As you learn the differences that make you and your partner individuals, and as you make compromises, you are creating new ways of doing things that work for your new family.

If You Are Looking for Trouble, You Will Always Find It
If you thought you could trust this person enough to get married, then why do you stop trusting the first time things don't feel right? Trust them when they say they are telling you the truth. Yes, it's possible that they are truly lying, and there are many examples of how lies and infidelity can damage a relationship, but don't look for it. (Don't look in pockets or pocketbooks, or check phone messages or Facebook pages, etc., just to catch your partner in the lie you believe is being told.)

On the other hand, don't ignore the signs that tell you something is wrong. If you notice a change in the pattern of behavior, ask first what it is about.

Please do not allow "the guys" or your "girls" to get involved by offering their thoughts and advice. This will often lead to trouble. As a matter of fact, don't even talk to them about what is bothering you. Your friends most often can only see your point of view. What is worse is that we complain when things are bad, so they don't even get to see both sides of the problem at all.

There is a concept in psychology that says: When you are around people who have the same feelings about a subject, in a group together, their beliefs become even stronger. What does that mean? You complain, your friends have been there before, so now they say, "Girl, I understand. I've got your back. He's a dog and you should leave his &$#%!"

However, the problem is... later you find out that he was telling the truth. You forgive him because you love him, and your friend is mad because she thinks you are being stupid. She is not in love with him; of course she will see things differently. So now that you have forgiven him, there is a strain in your friendship.

My advice: keep your problems to yourself. Trust only someone you KNOW can be objective (someone who can look at things from many angles, and most importantly, someone who can explain and explore both sides of the story. Remember, only take advice from a professional or from someone who was successfully married for eight years or more.

Forgiveness

The people whom we have to forgive the most in this world are often our parents, our siblings and our spouses. It is important for us to forgive, even if the past situation was a "bad thing."

Forgiveness heals. That is quite a powerful statement to think about. When you are hurt by someone you love, often we hold on to the thoughts and the feelings of that thing that he/she did that really hurt you. Those words go around and around and around in our minds—"I can't believe that she did that." "If he loved me, he would have never done that." The pain that was so intense when we found out what happened, starts to grow and grow every time we think about it. All this can happen within a few minutes or a few hours. Then if we do not challenge our thoughts or feelings, that disrespectful act becomes unforgivable... and unforgettable. How many times have you said, "I may forgive, but I sure will never forget." But what does that do for you? When you choose to never forget, you end up persecuting the person forever, for something that may have happened a LONG time before.

Everything that ever has and ever will happen to us on this Earth is a lesson to help our spiritual selves grow. If we are holding on to the pain, the blame, the hurt, the shame, we are not opening ourselves to love, peace and happiness. We cannot choose to live life's opposites at the same time; it doesn't work. We cannot choose peace and pain, at the same time. They are opposites and cannot exist in the same space and time, it doesn't work.

So do you choose to be happily married or do you choose to be ticked off because of the stupid things that you feel that he is doing? Is it more important to be happy or to be right? If he needs help to stop making stupid mistakes, find someone who can help him see things differently like his family. It is often easier to listen to our family than our spouses.

I recently went to a seminar on radical forgiveness (www.radicalforgiveness.com) with a life coach named Kym Kennedy. The concept behind radical forgiveness is that we should thank those people who brought us those challenges so that we can grow to be the person that God has intended us to become. If you look back at any "bad thing" that has happened, you can probably now see something that has come from it. (Even if it is only how to spot that behavior in someone else.) Most likely you have become stronger. Moreover, know that once you have survived one obstacle, you know that if there is another one, you can handle it even better.

I hear someone saying, "Should I forgive abuse?" Forgive it, yes; accept it, no way. If someone is abusive, you must thank them for the lesson and move away quickly. Do not allow yourself to be the punching bag, either by words or by action. You are God's special gift, and everyone you keep around you should treat you that way. If he is unable to do that, he needs help, let him find it, and in the meantime get yourself to safety.

Do not allow your children to learn that abuse is okay. It is not okay. The more you love yourself, the easier it is for someone else to love you. Make sure your words and your energy say, "I am lovable and deserve the best." I know that this is very hard, so please, if you are in this situation, seek professional help.

Loving Each Other and Helping Each Other Grow
I work with children often, and the first thing I tell them when I meet them is "I love you, and what that means to me is that I want what is best for you." Love is wanting to help each other grow so that you and your mate can be the best you can be. Sometimes that means that you have to go the extra mile for your mate.

Ladies, I know you may feel that you are already doing too much. How can you possibly be expected to do more? But sometimes we just have to (especially when you are the one who has it together). The world out there is not very supportive of African-American men, so we must make sure that we are. If that means we need to help them figure out what to do with their lives, help them write their resumes, find places to send it to, practice interviewing skills, whatever. If you have more professional skills than your mate, you have to help teach him and place him in the environments where he can catch up with you.

If you are lucky enough to have a man who is doing his thing professionally, you have to understand that may mean that his work may demand time that you think should be for you and the children. Don't get jealous of the time he is putting in at work when he is doing his thing. And when he comes home, let him know that you appreciate all he does outside of the house. Make his home as comfortable for him (nice words, nice food, good intimacy) so he won't have any need to look to someone outside of the house.

Men, if you are staying home because in today's troubled economy you can't find a job, try to help out in the house as much as you can. I am not saying to turn into the "housewife" and "compromise your manhood," but do what you can as a partner in the relationship to make things work. You may find that when she can come home to a meal, she may have more energy for you at nighttime, if you know what I mean.

When you are both working hard, you have a challenge of finding time for one another. You must make time to spend together, even if it means it is scheduled. Yes, that may feel artificial, but better that than feeling neglected. If you both have extra money, perhaps you can consider having someone do the cooking and cleaning so you can have more time to spend with one another.

Organize Yourself

Having children is a big commitment in a relationship, and one you can't take back. Make sure that when you start planning to have children, you are planning on how you will parent the children. Make sure that you agree on fundamental issues such as: what spiritual practice will be taught and how; what last name they will take (that sounds simple, but these days many women are choosing to keep their birth last name); how you will discipline (if you believe in corporal punishment and your mate doesn't, that is a recipe for many arguments); the issue of circumcising your sons; private school vs. public school vs. home school; what role you expect a mother to play, a father; how you will divide your time between the children and yourselves.

These are important things to think about and discuss. If you already have children, it is good to have the discussion now to minimize problems down the road, or just to clarify why you have been doing the things that you have been doing. This is especially important when one person already has children and the other is about to be an "instant parent." This requires lots of conversation and a lot of support.

It is hard on step-children to accept a new parental figure, so take your time with expressing your expectations for the children. Show them the love and the respect that will make them want to listen to you when it comes time for discipline. Let each partner do the disciplining of their own children at first until your new family is well established. I am not saying that you allow the children to disrespect you; nor am I telling you to just never discipline them in the beginning. Just be mindful of the delicate relationship that you have in the beginning.

You must work together to juggle all the responsibilities and still have time for each other. This bears repeating: When you have children, it is still important that you and your mate find some private time together. Find someone you can trust to watch the children, because even though you are mom and dad, you cannot forget to be husband and wife. "Date night" is important, whether it is once a week or once a month. It is important to have time to reconnect and remember what life was like before the children came into the picture.

Take Time for Yourself
This may be something that is really easy for some couples, and can be a problem for others. It is important to have time to yourself. Not only is it important, as was said earlier, to spend time together as a couple, it is also important to spend time by yourself. We need time to "recharge." This may look different for different people.

For the men, it may mean watching the game with the guys. For women, it may mean getting a manicure, lunch with the girls or taking a bubble bath. For each of you, it may mean time to exercise, to pray or meditate—whatever it is for you take some time for yourself to relax and get the energy to continue doing the things you need to do. These things are stress reducers, and everyone must have a way of reducing life's stress so that you do not bring that into your marriage. My only word of caution is, when you see your mate doing one of these things, and you think it is a waste of time or money, or it is time that he/she should be spending with you, recognize that there is worth in that time that your mate is alone or with friends, and that in the end, it will be important to your marriage.

Mental Health
This could be a long section, but I am keeping it brief. Understand that there are many men/women who may have psychological issues that affect their relationships, and no one may even realize it.

Men do not often show symptoms the way women do. The best example that I can think of is depression. When you think depression, you think, isolation, crying, sadness, not eating, sleeping too much. Now some of this is true for men, however often they do not cry or get sad. Depressed men will often become irritable, aggressive, behave recklessly, and may abuse alcohol and/or drugs.

They may be tired, have headaches or other pain, or loss of interest in things that used to be enjoyable. Men do not often want to admit to feeling depressed. They are not likely to want help because society often sees it as weakness.

Further, when men feel suicidal, it is more fatal than with women. In other words, women may make attempts, but men actually kill themselves at a much higher rate than women do, so please do take depression seriously. If you notice these tendencies, you may want to very sensitively have a discussion about it and come up with helpful working solutions. If someone is talking about killing themselves, it is very important to reach out to a trusted spiritual advisor, go to a hospital, or find other help immediately. It can save a life.

One word of caution—often as women, we think that our love can fix any problem. It CAN'T! Love does help to ease things, but it cannot make depression go away. No matter how good you treat him, depression—if it is clinical—it cannot just go away; don't think that you can make it better. If you want to help, find a professional who can help you to help him.

Conclusion

Marriage is not an easy adventure. It is a wonderful journey that is filled with ups and downs. Stay committed to making it work. The first few years are probably going to be a challenge, and do not be surprised if you feel like it is not worth it... often. But a successful marriage really is worth it. Stay committed to working on it. Make sure that you talk with each other about your expectations for the marriage and for each other. Use the floor and sponge technique so you can visually see whose turn it is to talk and when the listener can no longer hear any more information. If you find that you need help doing these things, see a professional counselor or other marriage expert. Do the work and stay married.

Betty H. Ali

Betty H. Ali is a Registered Nurse. She is originally from New York and started her career in 1989, when she received her R.N. from Queens Borough Community College. She worked in the ER Department at St. Joseph's Hospital in Flushing, New York.

She relocated to Atlanta in 1991 and has worked for St. Joseph's, South Fulton, Atlanta Medical Center, Grady Memorial and Decatur hospitals, specializing in intensive care. She has also worked for Odyssey Hospice. She is currently working on her M.A. degree.

Her interest in nursing was heightened when she observed young people dying due to a lack of understanding on how the mind, body and spirit are interconnected and work together, which brings about the equilibrium needed for balance and quality of life. This experience inspired her to offer a new approach to health and wellness, which inspired the formation of Compassionate Nurses, Inc. Mrs. Ali's husband, Brother Kareem, has been a successful entrepreneur for the last 20 years.

Dr. Chanda Pilgrim

Dr. Chanda Pilgrim, Holistic Counselor, received her doctorate in psychology from Fordham University. She has 15 years of experience working with children and adults with a wide range of behavioral issues, including ADHD, bipolar disorder, oppositional behavior, low self-esteem and depression. Dr. Pilgrim helps clients build internal strength through restructuring beliefs and using the science of breath. She can be reached by email at dr.c.pilgrim@gmail.com

References

Amato, P.R., DeBoer, D.D. (2001). The Transmission of Marital Instability Across Generations: Relationship Skills or Commitment to Marriage? Journal of Marriage and Family, 63 (4), 1038-1051.

Chakraburtty, A. (2009). Depression in Men. Retrieved from http://www.mayoclinic.com/health/male-depression/MC00041

Chapman, G. The 5 Love Languages. Retrieved from http://www.5lovelanguages.com

Chitwood, M. (2006). "What a Husband Needs From His Wife." Eugene, Oregon: Harvest House Publishers.

Cunny, Gloria (2004). Personal communication.

Rasheed, Sakinah, Ph.D, Psy.D. (2009). Personal communication.

Rogers, S.J., Amato, P.R. (1997). Is Marital Quality Declining? The Evidence From Two Generations Social Forces, 75, (3), 1089-1100.

Tipping, C. (2009). Radical Forgiveness. Retrieved from http://www.radicalforgiveness.com/

Discussion Questions

1. Review the Table of Contents. Analyze your relationship as it relates to the book.

_____

_____

_____

_____

_____

_____

_____

_____

_____

_____

_____

_____

_____

_____

_____

_____

_____

_____

_____

_____

_____

2. How could you improve your relationship?

_____

_____

_____

_____

_____

_____

_____

_____

_____

_____

_____

_____

_____

_____

_____

_____

_____

_____

_____

_____

_____

_____

_____

_____

3. Has God forgiven you of your faults?

_____

_____

_____

_____

_____

_____

_____

_____

_____

_____

_____

_____

_____

_____

_____

_____

_____

_____

_____

_____

_____

_____

_____

_____

4. Why should you forgive your mate?

_____

_____

_____

_____

_____

_____

_____

_____

_____

_____

_____

_____

_____

_____

_____

_____

_____

_____

_____

_____

_____

_____

_____

_____

5. What actions have you taken toward improving your relationship? Vital signs?

_____

_____

_____

_____

_____

_____

_____

_____

_____

_____

_____

_____

_____

_____

_____

_____

_____

_____

_____

_____

_____

_____

_____

_____

It's the man being in love with the woman, and the woman in love with the man. This, I think, is one of the prerequisites for a long-lasting marriage.

Printed in the United States
By Bookmasters